Becoming Mr. Right

Becoming Mr. Right

Steps You Can Take To Become The Best Version of Yourself for Yourself

By Eric Gillard

Becoming Mr. Right
Steps You Can Take to Become the Best Version of Yourself For Yourself

ISBN 978-1-4951-2754-0

10 9 8 7 6 5 4 3 2 1

Editing and design by Karen Morgan
Cover design by Matt Lawrence

New Lighthouse Media
Hampton, VA

Printed in the United States of America

Ne te quaesiveris extra

Contents

Prologue

When I first had the idea of "Becoming Mr. Right," it was originally set as a fiction novel called "Rebirth of a Romantic" and loosely based on my life so far. All the up and downs dramatized with the stirring dialogue, remarkable characters and deep plot development of a New York Times bestseller. Those plans were quickly dashed when I just couldn't focus on putting the words onto the page that would make the reader emotionally invested in the characters and their worlds.

So, during a lull at work, this book transitioned from one of fiction to reality as a self-help title. After all, the best stories are the ones that actually happened, right? Plus, I've learned that works of fiction take you away to a new world, but when you close the book or power down your smart device, your current situation returns to smack you in the face — the fantasy world dying to your present reality.

The best books I've remembered aren't works of fiction, even those that stir deep emotions and provoke numerous thoughts, but those that have given me practical and useful information to use in the betterment of my real life — Robert Greene's "48 Laws of Power," Dale Carnegie's "How To Wins Friends and Influence People," Napoleon Hill's "Think and Grow Rich," David

Deida's "The Way of the Superior Man," and Robert Glover's "No More Mr. Nice Guy" for example. I'm not saying this book will be among those classics, but I'd like to aspire to great things by documenting the ways I have continually improved myself over a certain time span.

Despite me calling this book a self-help book, it's more a self-construction work. To sound bold, "Becoming Mr. Right" is something of a clarion call for men and how society is changing the roles, expectations and definitions of what it means to be a man. Before a man can be of service to others, he must first be in service to himself. Service to self will lead to self-confidence and can be felt by others. Crafting a man of high value takes time, patience and a lot of trial and error to acquire the skills, standards, and magnitude that is needed to make it successfully in this world. The first step is always the hardest in any journey, and I hope with this book it becomes a little easier for you to plant that proverbial foot on the road you choose to take.

This book was not written alone and I had a team at my back — with some people I know and some I've never met outside the Internet. I'd like to thank my dad, whose patience, examples, and continued guidance help spur me on in my development as a man. For the men whom I've only met online, thank you. Relationship and race commentator and entrepreneur Tommy Sotomayor was the first man I met on my journey one late winter night on YouTube, and his discovery was the catalyst to finding other men of a similar nature — Tom Leykis, Elliott Hulse, Keith and Kevin Hodge, Patrice O'Neal, Bill Burr, Jefferson Bethke, Tony Gaskins Jr., and Jereme Ford, among others. Thank you for filling in the gaps that needed to be filled. I'd also like to thank my editor, Karen Morgan, for her knowledge and expertise in getting this book out to the public.

Lastly, I'd like to thank all the women who have touched my life in various ways for the examples they have set in my eyes. A special shout out goes to those women who are still in my life, and most notably, to the ones who left; those who deserted helped make this book possible. You all have left indelible impressions in what to look for, and more importantly what not to look for, in a woman.

1
Introduction

"This above all: to thine own self be true..."
— William Shakespeare

What is a man? Whose definition of that word takes precedent? Is a man someone who takes care of others? Is it someone who has a lot of resources at his disposal? Is it someone who is an example for other men to follow? Is it someone who can have sex with any woman he pleases? Is it someone who is well known among people you will never meet? Or is it someone who lives proudly and unashamedly by his own definition and on his own terms?

Derek Sivers, entrepreneur and founder of CD Baby, has a blog post on his website, www.sivers.org, which changed my way of thinking about empowerment and personal responsibility, and what it means to live your life — especially as a man.

The post, called "Everything is my fault," railed about the things that happened to him because of other people in his business dealings. He at first blamed the outside for the trouble he was under. But he realized that he put himself in that position by not taking charge of many situations to prevent unnecessary hardship.

By telling yourself that everything is your fault, it gives you total power of what happens to you — both good and bad. It was empowering, and I still refer to the blog post on occasion when I feel the need to soak up more information from a man with a bevy of varied life and business experience.

"Now you're like a new superhero, just discovering your strength. Now you're the powerful person that made things happen, made a mistake and can learn from it. Now you're in control and there's nothing to complain about," he wrote.

Telling yourself that everything is your fault is a new way of attaining personal responsibility and accountability — to yourself and to others. As a man, you are in the prime position of power. People watch what you do and what you say, and wait for your cues. Figuring out who you are, what you care about, what you believe in, and what you stand for are the most important, and most difficult, challenges of becoming a man. Outside influences can positively or negatively shape the frame of a man in many directions and cause him to shift from one cause or belief to another.

There is a price to be paid in becoming a man, and that price is constant vigilance. As a man, you are constantly bombarded with the expectations, fair and unfair, of others who try and steer you into their frame and their rationale of what a man should be. Societal pressure bends men to conform to what others want for themselves, not what you as a man want for yourself.

As a man, your happiness and fulfillment should always be independent of anything or anyone other than yourself. Remember that, as a man, you come first. If you constantly rely on external items or people for your happiness, then be sure to expect constant disappointment, strained relationships, high levels of frustration, and the nagging feeling of being unfulfilled.

Many men in this evolving society we live in are lost and looking for some greater cause, goal or tribe to belong to. Whether it's the peculiar fandom of a girl's cartoon show starring ponies, or supporting a professional sports team full of millionaires, or making noise anonymously on the Internet or even joining a gang, men have an eternal need and desire to belong to something greater than themselves — even if they have no personal mission that drives them. For better or worse, men need a structure to be a part of or build for themselves.

Not everyone you know aspires to become something greater than themselves — they just want to be average, be a part of the herd, make ends meet and blend in with the crowd. What kind of life is that? Why would you want that for yourself?

Before you were born, you didn't have a choice of your parents, where you were born, what race or genetics you were given, or what religion to believe. From then on, it's all about the choices you make. Wherever you are now exactly represents the sum of your previous decisions and actions.

As we grow and mature until the day we die, every day gives you new opportunities to choose — you can choose to live through the eyes of others or through your eyes. What you see depends on what you're looking for, of course. Are you looking for the approval of others and are willing to bend yourself to their whims based on the artificial confines they live in? Are you apt to "man up" to another's definition of what a man should be? Or are you looking to become a sovereign beacon for others to see and admire by having the courage to live a life true to yourself, not the life others expected of you? Self-improvement should be for you, not for anyone else.

The title of this book could be a bit misleading. The term "Mr. Right" is most often used if you are paired with your "Ms.

Right." My use of "Mr. Right" isn't in the vein of seeking a romantic relationship with another person, but with forging a relationship with you — the most important person in your life.

The most-often used piece of dating advice given to people, with well intentions, is to "be yourself." Well let me ask you, what if "yourself" is lacking in some area? What if "yourself" is tired of dealing with frustrations and disappointments? What if "yourself" has everything you want, except for what you want the most? If being "yourself" is not working, then you can't wait for other people to change and adjust to you — you need to change. Being yourself is only good enough when you're actively becoming the best version of yourself.

If something is broken, the time is now to fix it. If something is missing, the time is now to find it. If something is lacking, now is the time to fill it. If you are tired of making excuses and want real progress, the time is now. If you truly care about achieving your mission and goals, you won't have time to find excuses. If you want to become someone for others to admire, look within yourself to create the best version of you. The only person that can tell you what a man should be is you.

And for the women who happen to read this book, this book is meant for men. In the 21st century, manhood and the long, hard, cold process of developing to that level is slowly becoming an extinct ritual. Nowadays, most men come from broken families where the father was absent to teach his boy the ropes on the way to adulthood or he was physically present but didn't take charge as a man should do. As a result, men learned to put the women in their lives on a pedestal, and let our feelings run amok and emote under the slightest duress. A statement of warning against putting any woman on a pedestal: The man who places a woman on a pedestal should not be surprised when she looks down on him.

Also, societal changes have almost made being a man, and masculinity in general, a dirty, dangerous, shameful thing, as the previous roles men used to occupy are nearly gone or have been replaced. Without those roles and the men who occupy them to guide us, men are turning to new ways of becoming what a man should be in the current cultural state of affairs — all while women yearn for the way men used to be, the men that they claim to be searching for in their online dating profiles and in private conversations with their families and girlfriends.

Although these words are targeted for a male audience, women can take note on discovering your mission as well. However, men need purpose. Men need drive. Men need to forge their sense of being. Men need a vision to become the individuals they want to be and the men society need and requires of them. There's a statement I've coined that coincides with this: Women can be, men must become.

Women, if you are mothers, grandmothers, sisters, wives, fiancées, girlfriends, or just girls who happen to be friends of men, realize that men are still willing to be providers — they just need the right incentives and support to fulfill that role.

A woman can certainly be a strong force and can incentivize or discourage a man from becoming a provider — whether financially, physically, emotionally, spiritually, or through other resources. In the end, a woman, no matter the hierarchy level she is in a man's life, cannot change a man despite all her hopes and dreams nor should she want to — he has to change himself. In each phase of a man's life, the mission he chooses to go on has the potential to push him toward a new standard.

When it comes down to putting the money on the table, a man's goals, passion and most importantly, his mission, comes first. Everything else will fall into place — including a woman. Plus, a man becomes more attractive to a woman if he has a mission he is striving for and a goal of something bigger that he is going toward, right? Attracting a woman is a byproduct of the self, men: self-acceptance, self-development, self-love and self-respect. To quote comedian Patrice O'Neil: "Women don't want to win; they want to be with a winner."

Men, I hope this book will help spur positive changes in your life. The unique traits that make a man a man, such as strength, aggressiveness, fortitude, labor, decisiveness, pride and honor, are vilified and shamed in day-to-day life, the mainstream media, prime-time TV entertainment and Hollywood movies in tropes of dopey, fumbling, emasculated men, which is a shame. A return to the values and traits that make a man a man are sorely needed and subconsciously yearned for in today's society.

This book is written for me as well as for you, dear reader. As Italian astronomer and philosopher Galileo Galilei once said, "You cannot teach a man anything; you can only help him discover it in himself." I'm on my long path of self-discovery and self-construction.

Inspiration can come from the bright and dark spots in life; the point being that stimulus for men to re-evaluate and change their lives can come from many places. The power to change is in your hands and mind, men. It's never too late to get on the difficult but necessary road to your masculine side. Are you willing to make the necessary and tough decisions happen? Or will you sit back and let other people and outside forces make decisions for you and wonder in disbelief what happened to you? If you are ready to make the decision to improve, then the time is now to take the many but necessary steps to raise your value and become the best version of yourself.

2.

At a Crossroads

"Leave each man free to work out his own salvation."
— Arthur Schopenhauer

When things go wrong, sometimes the hardest image to look at is the one of you in the mirror. It can be unflinching, unforgiving and unrelenting. If you can't stand the reflection you see most days, you're not alone.

We men are our harshest critics when things don't go according to our well-laid plans — whether we lose a job, something of material value or someone near and dear to us. When loss strikes a man, which happens to all of us at some juncture in our lives, it truly is a measure of his inner steel. Usually, the most devastating events in a man's life can hold the most important lessons and opportunities for change.

The couldas, wouldas, and shouldas make their unwanted appearances when we fail. The sharp glare of introspection for men is white hot and unyielding — but is also the purest disinfectant for the reasons that cause failure in the first place.

My resolve was put to the test, like many a man's resolve has been under fire before, over a woman. Shame to say it's always over a woman, isn't it?

We men usually have this image of a "perfect" woman in our heads — a prototype that rarely comes to fruition outside our vivid imagination. Perfect is something that might work in theory but never in practice. One result of that fallacy is that we men falsely equate a woman's physical beauty to her perceived purity.

I'm sure you've dated your fair share of women that have disappointed the image that was front and center in your subconscious, which turned out to be a falsehood. Most of all, you're disappointed in the image of yourself.

When I broke up with a girl I was dating for more than two years, I couldn't look myself in the mirror for days on end. The end of our relationship began a downward spiral for me personally, which I call my "dark times."

I put on a brave face for my family, friends, and co-workers, but inside I was a mess. The girl I thought was "the one" for me — "the one" who I bought a ring for, "the one" who I would do almost anything for, "the one" that I wanted to move for — turned out to not be "the one" in the most basic sense of the romantic fallacy we visual creatures create for ourselves. I had a severe case of "oneitis," which was proven when I foolishly took her back after she cheated on me with a former college classmate of hers. The result of that "oneitis" was the painful extraction of the object of my misplaced desires and the scorched earth policy I had to apply.

All of my hopes, dreams and aspirations were wrapped up in her, which is a grave mistake to pin any semblance of a future to a person whether they know it or not. Boy, did I pay for that naïveté.

I had no self-esteem, because I did not know, or better yet

create, myself. I had a low sense of value because what I thought
I could offer a woman was totally wrong. I had a low sense of
self-worth because I was giving myself to others too cheaply.
After the breakup I was like an open sore, as painful and unre-
solved feelings from my past that I felt hampered my development as a man rose to the fore and needed to be reconciled.

After my breakup, the problem was that I was looking for
external validation, for someone to tell me everything was going
to be OK, as if I were still a little boy that needed his hand held.
I didn't get that; I got anger and frustration instead. Seeking
validation from others is an expensive and foolish endeavor and
only values their lives over yours — just ask the women who
love to take selfies and post them on the various social media
channels seeking approval from gawkers and thirsty, horny men.
I learned the hard way that if you live by someone's approval,
then you'll die by their rejection. It took me months to realize
that I needed to stop looking to the outside for hope, fulfillment,
and accomplishment, but to the inside.

I realized something was wrong with me and that only I can
fix what ails me. I'm still undergoing that healing process, and
I still slip up from time to time, but those dark times brought
me to the light of self-actualization and self-love where you are
constantly trying to improve yourself and your surroundings,
and the understanding that I never want to feel those feelings
of powerlessness and weakness I had during my breakup and
subsequent fallout.

When a man loses, it forces him to look inward — to reassess,
to recover, to reevaluate his stock and what he is able to gather
from the wreckage of defeat. He is placed at a crossroads — one
direction toward self-loathing, depression, hatred and apathy;
the other direction toward awakening, rediscovery, rebirth and
renewal.

I realized that the choice to control my destiny was mine —
not my parents, my siblings, my job, my address, my car, my
significant other or anyone or anything else. Everything that
occurs in my life, the good and the bad, is my fault. Everything
that happens to you, men, is your fault whether you want to admit that or not. You cannot fix a problem or foster a positive life
by placing the blame on others, which was a mistake I made too
often. Playing the victim is a guarantee for failure. Losers visualize the penalties of failure, and winners visualize the rewards
of success.

Who you are, where you are, what you are doing and what
you have are been administered by you. If your life is not satis-
fying, the questions you need to ask yourself are: Do you have
the courage and aptitude to change it for the better? Are you
willing to transform the biggest moments of pain, disappointment and hardship into something good?

You can choose the path of wallowing or of persevering.

Men, if you are reading this book, you have chosen the second
path when things went awry and decided to press through the
pain — the path toward overcoming your failures, not accepting
the role of a victim, rising above your circumstances, and making sure it never happens again. Instead of letting things happen
to you, men, you have the power to choose what happens to you.

In a classical English class in university, my English professor
told me and the rest of her class that when she reads papers, one
question must be answered about any conclusions raised: "So
what?" I put that comment away at the time, but it's a profound
query to pose. So what if a man gets his heart broken? He must
wipe off the dust and continue forward. So what if relationships
with family are strained? He must empower himself to fix them
himself or cut ties. So what if he is bored and uninterested at
work? He must grin and bear it or begin the search for new

employment. So what if he is unsatisfied in life? He must look within himself to rectify what's wrong or he can wallow in pity like a pig in the mud.

We can get easily attached to titles and people. When those are cut from you, it's almost like losing a part of your body. Losing an attachment hurts like an amputation of a limb or the loss of a bodily organ. Men easily get wrapped up in the external trappings of labels — through romance, through work, through family, through friendships, through money. All of those brands can help define a man, but they also can trap a man into looking outside himself for validation and purpose. When the external titles crash in a steaming heap, the internal is exposed for the entire world to see — and sometimes it's not a pretty sight.

External titles are merely props in our lives; they should not encompass your entire life. Titles and trophies are not important in the long run. What is important is who we are on the inside. A man's validation and purpose must come from within, to build something he and only he can appreciate and provide satisfaction over all outside elements. A man's mission must be his life's work, his calling, his drive to succeed and contribute his unique gifts to the world.

The life you live is best lived in a straight, clear, focused manner. Whatever mission you choose to pursue — whether it's sports, writing, public service, religion, entertainment or fitness, for example — the steps you take in your life must head toward that chosen direction.

The Rev. Martin Luther King Jr. had a calling. Steve Jobs had a drive. Thomas Edison had a mission. Henry Ford had a goal. Nelson Mandela had a purpose. All men must have that hunger, lest face his own demise.

This mission must be something you believe in and can pursue with purpose and passion.

                                          Becoming Mr. Right

The problem is that finding your mission in life doesn't just fall from the sky.

Men today who direct their energies toward a personal and purposeful mission are the rarest breed around.

I don't claim to be a self-help guru or a life coach and I'm not a certified psychologist or psychiatric — I'm just a man who is looking to build and grow in an ever-changing world. This book can hopefully provide you tools in your journey. But make no mistake, men — you must put in the hard work to get the results you want.

With this book, I hope to tell you a little bit more about my continuing journey and how it can help you become the best man you can be — for yourself.

If you don't have anything to give to the world that is of benefit, if you cannot be Mr. Right to others, how can you possibly be Mr. Right to yourself?

Your mission should be your highest priority — everything else will flow into its proper place in your life from there. You cannot be your true self by denying your mission and what it takes to achieve it. Your mission in life is a reflection of your character, habits and attitude. The decisions that you make from this point forward will make you who you are, as your actions flow from the inside. And like anything a man accomplishes, he must start small before he can go big.

3.
Starting Small

"Most people have achieved their greatest success just one step beyond their greatest failure."
— Napoleon Hill

Sometimes you have to hit rock bottom before you can start climbing toward the life you want for yourself. If that's you now, or at any stage in your life, this is the time to build yourself into the man you wanted to be. It is time to be selfish. This is the time to do exactly what is best for you, not what's best for everyone else. It's time to go after what you want. If you do not step forward, you will always be in the same place you are. Doing nothing gets you nothing.

If you're staring up from the bottom of your proverbial hole, the only place you can go is up, right? Yes, that is the lamest of clichés — but clichés are true for a reason.

Your first inclination isn't to jump out of the hole like a super hero, but to see what small section of rock you can use to slowly traverse upward. Some people lean on their religious faith as their rock, others their educational background or life experienc-

Becoming Mr. Right

es, or close family and friends — whatever your rock is, use it.

At my lowest point, after a period of useless self-loathing and self-doubt, I used a collection of the above "rocks" to start small toward my recovery. Finding people, whether in real life or on the Internet, who have gone through similar situations also helped steer me toward a breakthrough.

When you're broken down, the first steps aren't to take all the strewn-about pieces and try to rebuild all at once — it must be done little by little, brick by brick, piece by piece. Start with the basics, and then keep adding until you get what you want. When you've been at your worst points, you never want to go back there. That's what should keep you focused. There are no short-cuts on your way to creating your best self.

Think of it this way: Imagine yourself as the owner of a sports team that is constantly underachieving season after season. You might want to fire the head coach and totally clean house, or spend a lot of money to bring in a high-priced free agent to help right the ship. Those teams that are unstable at the top rarely succeed. Steady, patient ownership with knowledgeable staff at every level breeds consistent victory and championship results. The goal of any sports franchise is to win a championship, and every player, coach, high-level executive and staff member must have the singular mindset for success. You are either climbing toward success or sliding toward failure — there is no in-between.

In order to start small, you must look at the things that can be fixed — some are more obvious than others. Some examples: a new job can help alleviate your financial situation, changing your diet by replacing unhealthy food and drink with healthier alternatives, cutting out people in your life that are takers and not givers can work wonders for you. Remember — you are in charge of your life, especially as a man, which you should have total dominion over. Taking charge will be a key topic in this book, so please make a note of it as it will be attributed throughout. If you don't take initiative, you probably will not get much of what you want, if anything, in life. If you're not consciously and consistently working toward improving your station in life, you're basically surviving, not living.

Also with starting small is starting how you define your success. My success will undoubtedly be different than yours. What you think is important regarding your priorities and how you organize them is a statement about your character. What are you trying to accomplish in your path of self-improvement? Are you aiming to be better with romantic relationships? Do you need to be a better family man? Are you focusing on improving your business/financial outlook? Are you just wanting to be a more confident and sure person? Your version of success will be your own — no one else's. Keep that in mind when you begin to build the best version of yourself.

How you define success can greatly influence how you go about getting it. If you want to be an award-winning novelist, following in the footsteps of the president of a Fortune 500 company will be a terrible archetype to emulate. When learning how to achieve your goals and desires, you are the only person who can define what success looks like for you, so go forth and take the small steps toward your results. Without a why, things can't happen in your favor.

Starting small doesn't necessarily mean having small goals, it means having a laser-like focus to set one goal and accomplish it. It is very hard to do many things well due to the time needed to devote to each area; in this instance, the only thing that should be a Swiss Army Knife is a Swiss Army Knife.

It is much easier to do one thing well as you won't be distracted and flighty. Have your one mission, goal or objective

                                                    Becoming Mr. Right

and focus on it until your satisfaction. It should consume everything you think about and everything you do. Make a decision to figure out what you and only you want, and then pursue that with passion. Take one small step toward the goal every day, as you will never leave your current station in life until you make conscious choices to go where you want to be.

In branching off the process of taking small steps, keep this acronym paramount in your mind and heart: K.I.S.S. — Keep It Simple, Stupid. There is no need for a complex set of rituals or robotic memorization, as complexity can become a needless barrier to your success. Making a simple goal complex doesn't help you achieve it any faster or better. Just do something small and simple — every day. It's all about making small changes and being consistent in that new scope of behavior. Little by little and piece by piece, progress will be made.

If you take small, simple steps every day in your mission, you would accomplish it before you know it. The line between an achiever and a failure is a small step above the proverbial line. Every action you take should bring you one step closer to your goal. As a bonus, taking those steps every day could be a catalyst to changing your behavior for the good. The process of positivity will become a part of who you are as your daily actions will turn into a lifelong habit that you won't want to break.

This book is my example of starting small. I'm a journalist by trade, but I was taken off reporting due to staffing issues, so my writing, which is my mission, took a back seat professionally. This small step I'm taking with this book is me getting back to doing what I love to do and what fulfills me when no job, friendship, family member, or woman can. I couldn't let a professional setback become a personal one. The only entity that is stopping you from living the life you want to live is you.

Every mission, goal and aim you have comes down to one

simple step: The first step. If you want to lose weight, you need to make the step by working out or fixing your diet. If you want to make more money, you need to make the step in creating a business or look for more gainful employment. If you want to be better with women, you need to make the step to talk to them every day — whether in person or online. If you want a better relationship with your children, then you need to make the step to get to know them and see how they operate independent of you. If you want to make more money, learn from financially successful people.

As soon as you have a mission that you believe in, start immediately taking your first small steps toward personal fulfillment and satisfaction. Remember, men: It's never too late to become what you want to be.

While your mission or goal can be simple, the execution of it is what matters — and that is where you, as a man, must recognize and appreciate your unique gifts and abilities.

4.
Know Your Gifts

"Whatever you are, be a good one."
— Abraham Lincoln

As men, we think critically and analytically about every situation we are in — or at least we should. The only thing stopping you from changing yourself is changing your mindset to do better, and that's where your natural gifts and abilities come in.

Going back before my "dark days," I allowed myself to be immersed in the opinions and thoughts of others, hanging on their words and opinions to see if I was worthy of their approval or validation. That was a mistake that nearly turned grave, as I contemplated suicide — suicide not only in taking my own physical life, but wanting my current life to die and a new one to somehow take its place.

I felt stuck with no future personal prospects to keep me going. I thought of swallowing a bottle of sleeping pills chased with a bottle of bourbon or diving off a bridge into the water or driving my car into oncoming traffic on the highway, all because I had a mental and spiritual death. I was the definition of a scared, frustrated chump. But instead of killing myself, I decided to kill the negative thoughts, beliefs and mindset that was holding me back.

There's no need to look outside for validation or recognition of what you have inside. Stop waiting on other people to give you what equipment you can freely and unconditionally give yourself. Give yourself permission to be enough for you and let others see for themselves.

We all have something we are good at, whether we know it or not. My dad always told me that men must be in service to others. He was implicitly suggesting that in the service of women, which is fine but only to those who have proven themselves and their value to you and are worthy of your gifts. But before you serve anyone else, you must be in service to yourself.

When I speak of gifts, I speak of unique qualities and abilities you can do that not everyone else can do. Are you curious about what you can excel? Do you wonder at what professions you could do great? Your gifts and talents define the tasks, jobs and lifestyle at which you have the natural ability to be great. When you tap into or develop your innate abilities you can achieve amazing results.

Each of your gifts and talents represent an ability to do, sense, be aware or know something. You need to know what you are able to do, and you've got to be honest with yourself about what you are not able to do. And while you might not be able to list them off the top of your head, you have at least a handful of abilities that are as much a part of you as your unique physical features.

Also ask yourself these questions in your exploratory phase, men: What gives me life? What excites me? What am I naturally curious about? What makes my heart beat a little faster than my normal speed? Write them down in any format, like a diary

                              Becoming Mr. Right

or a bullet list — you choose.

Please note, I didn't say to ask yourself what makes you happy. Happy is a word that gets thrown around too often and is taken too lightly. Happy is a feeling that can be as fleeting as a summer's breeze, just like its opposite but equal-in-impact feeling of sadness. Remember that happiness doesn't always make you "feel" happy. Here's an equation to remember: happiness equals reality minus undue expectations. With that in mind, in order to obtain your version of happy, you must first define what it is for you. Based upon your definition, you might find the need to redefine your happy in order to possess, obtain and maintain it.

Contentment should be the precursor to your happiness, and when you are working in your mission, that should bring true happiness. Things that give you life will fulfill and sustain you. Things that give you life will give you a meaning in life. Things that give you life wake you up in early in the morning and keep you up late at night. Things that give you life cannot be co-opted by anyone or anything.

As men, our talents are usually recognized only when they benefit others; they are one of the things that make us unique and special. However, I want you to flip the script and use your gifts to your benefit first and foremost. Only if someone is worthy of receiving your gifts (family, significant other, close associates, etc.) is it OK to give of yourself. You are the only person who has your set of unique gifts and talents for potential success. Pay attention to the things you are good at and like to do to begin to find your gifts.

But knowing your gifts doesn't mean just focusing on your positives. The process of finding your gifts is also a time to spotlight your negatives. Every person, whether they like to admit it nor not has some flaws, and there's nothing inherently wrong with that. The issue with negatives becomes when they begin to take over the rest of a person's behavior and thought process. Spotlight your weaknesses and work to make them your strengths. If you choose to focus on fixing your negatives, use the energy in that to forge an opportunity to cultivate a deeper mindfulness and understanding of yourself.

So, men, what do you like to do when no one is looking? Do you enjoy building or fixing things with your hands? Are you analytical and like to deal with numbers? Do you have a hobby that you'd like to make into something more? Do you have a fondness for charities? Are you more apt to communicate with something other than words, or are you a wordsmith?

I challenge you to take a critical look at yourself, assess your natural talents and recognize each gift you have and write down what you are going to do with each one, even seek counsel from people you trust and respect if need be. You can give yourself some proverbial goal posts with these questions: "What else haven't I thought of?" "What comes so natural to me that I haven't thought of writing it down?" and "If I had more things to write down, what would they be?"

Your gifts and talents are such that should inspire you and make you feel that you have a basic understanding of the things you are powerful at and the passions you hold dear. Passion is a concrete consideration which tends to speaks to natural talent and innate drive. Follow your passion and it will lead you to finding your mission. However, in order to get what you want, you must first know and find what it is that you want.

5.
Finding Your Mission

"It always seems impossible until it's done."
— Nelson Mandela

When it comes to your mission, you have to name it before you can claim it, so get clear about what you want and take action toward it. Not knowing what you want — from your major life goals to your day-to-day desires — is not acceptable. Closed mouths don't get fed. If you don't even know what you want, then you can't even ask for it.

Power is the beginning and end of everything as a man, especially over you. The goal of finding your mission is to strive to be self-sufficient in all areas of your life so you can draw closer to yourself and others as a result; to accept yourself, and therefore expect more of yourself and others.

Some people don't realize their aptitudes, either through ignorance or lack of ambition. One key to finding your mission is to discern what draws you in. What do you already excel at? Then find a mission that maintains that excellence. What are you competent at? Do what it takes to elevate that competence into excellence in your chosen mission. What am I not good at? Do what it takes to achieve competence in that area. Knowing the things that grab your attention will help you determine that. Everything you do from now on must be from a position of strength and knowledge, not of weakness and ignorance.

One aspect of finding your mission is trying different things out. You wouldn't go to a clothing store and buy the first pair of pants you see, would you? You try them on and see if they are a good fit for your body and your wallet. The same parable can be transferred to finding your mission. Don't be afraid to sample things out to see what you are great at — this means you must try many things. If one thing doesn't suit you, drop it and move on to the next. If one mission won't work for you, find another mission. We all get knocked down and disappointed, but it's essential to get back up and go again.

Your mission rarely involves doing the same thing your entire life. That might sound odd, but as with anyone, our interests can change from time to time or if you acquire new life experiences. For example, Ronald Reagan was a famous Hollywood actor before he had higher aspirations that lead him to become the President of the United States. Harland Sanders, better known as Colonel Sanders of KFC fame, was a railroad worker, among other things, before getting into the fried chicken business. George Foreman was the heavyweight champion of the world in boxing before being known for the "lean, mean grilling machines" that bear his name in the kitchens of many homes worldwide.

You're looking for something that makes you feel a deep sense of satisfaction with your life. Keep trying things out that will work for you. Once you have found it, don't second guess yourself. It's OK if others don't understand how this could be your life purpose. It's OK if you can't explain to others why it feels so right for you. As long as it works for you, that's all that matters. You should have a life of "oh wells" as opposed to a life of "what ifs." Don't be afraid to start over, too; it can create a brand-new opportunity to attain what you truly desire.

A man should have complete and total control over his mission, but his mission must follow some essential guidelines to ensure success:

- It should be actionable

All potential missions should be written down like you were making a grocery list. Start with a blueprint to define your goals, then be as detailed as you can be about making your mission a reality and taking the necessary steps. When it comes to the nitty gritty, it always comes down to taking action. You can study as much theory as you'd like, but any acquired or ingrained knowledge is useless without you taking action. Cultivate the essential mindset that if you don't keep moving and growing you'll start to die, not only in the physical sense but in the spiritual sense. Inaction equates to death, and that's why your mission must be feasible. With that being said, turning your ideas into action isn't always a straightforward process like you would hope. You should set of proverbial yard markers as a guide.

- It should be quantifiable

This doesn't mean to make it a numbers game or an equation where you have to hit A-B-C before X-Y-Z happens. This means that while in the course of your mission, you must be able to track certain obtainable marks. For example, if your goal is to work in the fitness industry, you need to get certain qualifications and certificates. Or if you want to become better in the kitchen, you can tell yourself to cook a certain flavor of dishes, like Italian or vegetarian, before moving on to the next culinary discipline. The utility in building the resume of your mission is more paramount than some arbitrary numbers. Make your mission feasible by breaking it down small that you can take it step by step, as stated in Chapter 3. Tracking your successes can help in two ways: spurring you on to motivate you to keep going and to give you solid feedback on your efforts and whether something is working or not. Record your progress in little bites or stages, if need be.

• It should be reasonable

There's inherently nothing wrong with trying to obtain goals that some might classify as unreasonable, but the chances of failing and quitting are higher than your goals are. It's OK to be bold and shoot for the moon, but be bold without being unrealistic. Don't overload yourself with expectations and realize that movement in your self-improvement journey is a slow, deliberate process. There are only so many hours in a day, days in a month and months in a year. This is not an indictment against making your mission realistic, but your mission should work for you in the realm of your specific personal gifts. Know your limits and work around them as best you can. It's OK to have long-term goals, but achieving short-term successes are the bricks that need to be laid down first in forming the foundation to build your successful house.

• It should be relatable

Some missions are more obvious than others. Some are more obscure than others. Making your mission relatable is all about ease of adoption in line with your gifts. If you can't do something, are you willing to go against the grain and forge ahead despite the path being a difficult one? Or will you use what you know you can do to translate those gifts into a mission? With status in any mission comes respect and pride that can be seen and felt by others. Plus, you have the power to make anything you do cool and exciting given your passions and gifts.

• It should be yours

Everything you are should be an example of a living, breathing, walking and talking advertisement of your mission. Just like a person of faith in a divine being, or lack thereof, is a billboard of their way of life for outsiders to see, so are you with your chosen path. No outside forces can muster the strength to put your mission asunder. You might have setbacks, delays, and defeats, but the desire that fuels your passion will safeguard against any permanent defeat. Know your aim and refuse to let anyone steal your mission. And ask yourself this question, men: Are you willing to work harder than everyone else so you can live unlike everyone else? It's only when you start making choices for yourself that you will start living your mission your way.

The above principals are rooted in experimentation and trial and error. Try something new and see what happens — either positive or negative. The greatest experiment is nearly always done solo; gaining confidence in an area in your life is usually done best by yourself initially. Experiment with your own time, your own money and your own efforts. Yes, it can get expensive, but it's more honest and sincere. The cheap, dishonest experiment is to use other people's energies, other people's resources, and other people's bodies as if they were your personal science experiments.

Once you find a mission to your liking, go all out in it. Do not half-step in your walk, go for broke. It takes a commitment, a word many people do not understand or practice with much regularity. It takes a slow and deliberate transition to make your mission worthwhile to you, like creating a new habit. A strong habit of courage in all aspects of your life will help you greatly in your mission.

Once you know what you want to do, you have many ways to transition from whatever you're currently doing with your life to your mission. You can keep doing what you're doing, but do more of what you love and less of what you don't enjoy, you can keep working a side job while you slowly transition to your mission, you can quit everything and just make the big leap or you can keep working a side job.

Whatever you choose to do, that is the start of creating the domain you mission will live and thrive in for you and others to see.

                                            Becoming Mr. Right

6.
Creating Your Domain

"The first step toward success is taken when you refuse to be a captive of the environment in which you first find yourself."
— Mark Caine

Finding your mission is not a quick and easy matter — it takes time. Even more important than time, it takes focus and a new mindset. An oft-used phrase that populates self-help seminars is, "Your attitude determines your latitude." Is it catchy? Yes. Does it sound a bit too New Age? Maybe — but it's true. You can choose to be bitter about your circumstances or choose to get better mentally to change your situation. The first place to create your domain is in your mind before anything can be actuated physically.

You need not wait for anyone's permission or approval to change your attitude and how you think about yourself. Begin the process to change your mindset immediately. Any activity, positive or negative, flows from how you identify yourself.

Start redefining how you classify yourself. For example, if your mission is to become an actor, begin to call yourself one. It's not pumping your head full of hot air — it's creating a sense of obedience to yourself and to your mission. Identify to yourself who and what you are and what you want to become and then classify yourself as such.

Your focus and mindset are essential to the process, but something else is vital — pride. Pride is such a subjective term, bound to the intent of your actions and your level of satisfaction; you can be proud of an effort you give during a pick-up basketball game in a losing effort but not proud of the way you might have acted when you successfully bedded a supermodel.

Think of domain as the vehicle in which your mission will go. If you own or lease a vehicle, you would take as the best possible care of it inside and out. Every issue or breakdown of your vehicle gets resolved quickly before it becomes a major, expensive repair, or at least it should, given your available resources. The same principals should be applied to creating the vessel your mission will live.

You should also build a domain around your mission you can be proud of. When a person dies, their titles, honorifics and worldly accomplishments can be put on display for all to see on their tombstone of grave marker.

To put it in a sports context, do you want your mission's accomplishments to be displayed on a large video screen with pride and confidence? That is a true hallmark of a mission if it can be displayed with pride and passion.

Would you want this mission linked with your name for all eternity and etched onto your tombstone when you die? If it isn't something you are excited to talk to people about or sign your name to, it is not a fulfilling mission. If you feel a strong pull to do something under the cover of anonymity, it really isn't your mission.

Pride is also a reflection of your principals. I can't tell you what yours are, but they are embedded deep within you. One man's principles may be the opposite of another man's.

Whatever principles you have are yours. and you should be true to them. After my break up, I was searching for answers when I stumbled upon pick-up artists and the principals surrounding "game" on the Internet.

Many of the blogs I read advocated using game in the vein of pick-up artistry just for quick sex, not to craft more successful relationships with women. That's fine for some men, but initially that was not what I was going for. I wanted to create better relationships with women, not to just solely chat them up for a quick lay and then never talk to them again. I wanted long-term success, not just short-term pleasure.

I searched for other "game" blogs that weren't just about quick sex with sub-standard women, but about using game as a tool for self-improvement and taking your destiny in your own hands. Dressing better, eating cleaner, working out consistently, creating multiple streams of revenue, being more aware of your surroundings, and fostering new ways to interact with people is the game I chose to absorb myself in. I found those blogs and still read them on occasion. I use game to reclaim myself from others and create my domain — and to craft myself in an image I can be proud of.

If you try to pursue a mission that goes against your principles, your body will physically reject it. You won't be able to do it with passion, and for efforts will not lead to fulfillment. Find your principles and go from there.

What are your core principles? Do they revolve around family? Children? Religion? Sex? Public service? Money? Power? Music? Art? Communications? Travel? Volunteering? Know them and you can start to build you mission's domain. Once in a while, check your intentions and ask yourself why you are doing what you are doing and ask yourself if that's a good reason to do it. It's always good to check your intentions before you act on anything, when you look deep within yourself for the reasons to why you do the things you do. Your thoughts affect who you are and more importantly how you act.

Another issue that could starve your mission is with the work it takes for your mission, you might get bored with it. That's a natural phase that must be overcome. The wherewithal to push past any boredom you might encounter is a trademark of living your mission — however long it takes. Creating the domain that staves off boredom over any lack of progress or general malaise can make or break your outcome. If you are passionate about your mission, you should never get bored with it. In order to get great at anything, you need to immerse yourself in it. You need to put in the work, and you need to be diligent. So many people expect to get good at something without putting any real amount of time into it. There is no magic pill in creating a successful domain.

The domain in which your mission lives might also geographically take you to a new place on the map. Not all missions can be accomplished close to home, sometimes you need to leave the comforts and perceived safety net of home to venture out to your destiny. Be willing and ready to go to the beaches of Brazil, the temples of Japan, the deserts of Egypt, the mountains of Canada, or the castles of Germany — wherever it takes, you must be able to go. Thanks to the democratizing effect of the Internet, you can read just about anything on any topic by any writer in your workplace, your home, or in the palm of your hand.

All of the previous information in this chapter is about attaining personal growth — physical, mental, fiscal, etc. Growth in

                                              Becoming Mr. Right

any aspect is all about forcing yourself out of your comfort zone, doing the hard and necessary things and behaving in a different manner, because expansion cannot be accomplished otherwise. If you're comfortable with any challenge in front of you, then it's not outside your comfort zone. Challenge yourself to do the hard tasks to cultivate growth and competence.

Going back to the vehicle theory in this chapter, when you swerve or drift into the lane occupied by another vehicle, you increase the chance of getting into an accident. When you are in the process of creating your world, it's important to keep your focus forward and not to your proverbial sides that could be occupied by other people driving toward their mission.

7.
Staying In Your Lane

*"A good man lives in harmony with himself—
he neither seeks nor needs external approval."*
— Chin-Ning Chu

The world is full of people who aim to do the least amount of work in hopes of getting maximum results. That is pure folly. What is also folly is other people judging what you are doing purely out of spite or willful ignorance.

There's a saying in the African-American community that has gained popular acceptance: "Stay in your lane." What it means is to mind your own business; keep moving straight ahead and don't veer over into the personal affairs of others without their permission.

Some people who know you might give you advice, solicited or not. Listening to people's advice doesn't always mean taking it. You have to decide which advice is right for you. Just like it's their prerogative to provide their two cents, it's your prerogative to accept it or reject it.

Never base your life on the "shoulds" or "ought tos" of others — those are very defeatist attitudes, even if they are coming from people who believe your path is the right one. Why live a life trying to make someone else fulfill their definition of "happy?" It's your life to live as you see fit, not theirs. Only you can drive the lane you are on, which was constructed just for you.

It is important to recognize that if you do have doubters, they come from a place of lack and scarcity. A majority of the people who willfully and purposely interfere in your affairs had their dreams dashed in some form or fashion. Don't let someone who gave up on their dreams talk you out of yours. If someone isn't happy with themselves, chances are you should not expect them to be genuinely happy for you.

Be independent of the good and bad opinions of others as they will only get in your way. Everyone will have an opinion on your affairs, but not many will bring solutions or improvements. People should spend less time trying to mess with someone else's life and more time trying to better their own life. When others see you're cool and enjoying your life the way you see fit, they can go out of their way to try to interfere with the progress of your mission all they want, but their words and actions will not hamper you.

If the doubters in your life are family, which can be a bitter pill to swallow, don't use any discord to burn a bridge — just let them pay a higher toll to cross to your world, so to speak. Sometimes, the people in your family who say they love and care about you and want you to succeed can be your biggest enemies; they even might subconsciously want you to fail so you can stay with them.

You will have naysayers. You will have doubters. You will

have haters. Never mind them! You're under no obligation to explain yourself to people who aren't working as hard as you are. Don't expect strangers or family members who don't know the direction of their lives to give you the guidance you need to affirm yours. Sometimes you can't expect people to understand how you move in your mission when they haven't been privy to your vision. Ignore the boo birds — they usually come from the cheap nosebleed seats of life.

So many people focus on what you can't do, but with your focus, men, it's amazing what you can find when you focus on what you can do. It's much easier to follow your own mission than it is to follow the mission someone else wants for you. Have the courage to live a life true to yourself, not the life others expect of you.

Most people, whether a stranger, friend, family or foe, live their lives worrying about what other people will think of them. Why should you care about their opinions? No matter what, you will be sure to have critics and nitpickers to contend with. Life is too short and your mission too critical to worry about those who wish to bring you down. Don't change who you are, your mission, or the path you are on to please someone who has no bearing or investment in your goals and dreams. A hallmark of an educated mind and a driven man is to be able to entertain the thoughts and opinions of those without a vision without accepting them.

When you don't accept the unwanted opinions of others, it's also important to not do the same to others. You should spend less time trying to mess with someone else's life and more time trying to better your life. Men don't get in the affairs of others unless extraneous circumstances call for it. Most of the time, running interference in another person's life is needless and can be construed as petty and childish.

Staying in your lane is a belief in yourself and the direction
you are going. When you are on the path of your mission, there
will be distractions that might veer you off course. In the face
of any distractions, an urge to give them more than a passing
glance could be fatal.

Belief is staying true to yourself in the face of opportunities to
compromise your integrity. On your journey, there will be many
temptations to abandon the way of your mission that is true to
you. You and only you must believe in the patience required
to stay on the right road, and to defeat any opponents who ask
you to do it their way because they allegedly know better than
you, and they think their way will be easier and less demanding.
Don't fall for those traps! They haven't been given the vision required to travel on the road you are on, so you can't expect them
to give you the right directions to your end result.

If you choose to discuss your mission with others, you will
know who is on your side when you meet the people who truly
speak to your mission and not away from it. Belief is staying the
course long enough to find these people or to be found by them.
Belief is knowing what you are going to do, how you are going
to do it and acting upon it. There is no other path apart from the
one you have decided for yourself — regardless of the obstacles
that might try to obstruct you.

Staying true to the road you're going on means believing in
yourself and disallowing any distractions from others to impede
your progress. Be you no matter what. Don't let the misplaced
ideas of others, of what you should be and the idle chatter of ignorance change who you are. And most of all don't be ashamed
of what you are becoming, if you know the path you are on is
best for you and not hurting anyone else.

Although you start to take this trip alone, many have surely
blazed a path for you to travel. In this current climate, finding

knowledge that you can use is easy to obtain from many sources
and may just help you on your journey.

8.
Obtaining Knowledge

"Go to bed smarter than when you woke up."
— Charlie Munger

Famous Greek philosopher and physicist Aristotle is a man of many quotes and sayings. One such saying applies to this chapter: "All men by nature desire knowledge."

With the Internet being in the palm of your hand, knowledge is at your fingertips so you don't have to go to a faraway land unless you absolutely want to. The Internet is a great source of knowledge and inspiration for men; it's like a multi-story library. It is vital though that once you learn something, you go and apply that knowledge in your life. And having the proper information at hand is imperative in any successful mission. The man who really aims to be educated, who intends to know via as many sources as possible, is going to stay with his mission until it is complete.

You can first consider the knowledge you already have inside. They are the things you have done over and over in your life; so much so they became second nature. Sometimes that's a good thing, sometimes it's a bad thing. It is incumbent upon you to re-evaluate the information you are in possession of and see if it is compatible with your mission. If so, carry on. If not, cut it out.

A man knows how to educate himself in the course of his mission. Knowledge is an essential element in the success of your mission. There are bound to be plenty of people who have laid a well-trodden path in the course of your mission. But there's a trick to finding those from whom you wish to learn. You must choose them for the reasons that align with your values and your mission. Find people, either in person or on the internet, that embody the values that you want to have, not solely for the results they have achieved.

When we are born, we are naturally inquisitive children on the road to adulthood, always asking our parents or family members the whos, whats, whens, wheres, whys and hows. Adults are quick to stamp out any inquests they deem unfit. When we become adults, in the case of your mission, a return to that childish mindset of information seeking is not a regression, but a progression.

As stated in the end of Chapter 3, to achieve your mission, it would be wise to seek information from those who have successfully carved a path you wish to take. You aren't seeking validation that you are going on the right path, but gleaning knowledge from those who have gone before. There is nothing new under the sun, so seek the breadth of wisdom that is out there.

A simple way to get ahead in life, or in anything for that matter, is to associate with people who are better than you at something. Despite all the progress you might make, someone is always better than you at something. One person can be physically stronger than you, or smarter than you, or richer than you, or better-traveled than you. Rare is the person who you are equal with in nearly every facet of life.

Don't be ashamed to go under the proverbial learning tree if you see someone doing better than you in your chosen mission, whether they are your elders or contemporaries. If they see something in you and choose to drop some knowledge your way, listen and observe them with full attention and respect. You can't learn much through talking; your ears will never get you in trouble. You can learn many things from what anybody has to say and what you observe — you just have to pay attention. You have two ears, two eyes and one mouth for a reason — don't forget that.

People don't have to help you in any way, mind you. If they do, humility and respect can go a long way to gain knowledge based on the experiences of others. And when you are conversing to those you trust and admire, given them your full attention. That creates a bond that can be strengthened.

Does all this sound simple? Yes — it sounds simple because it is simple. Remember, men — K.I.S.S., and don't forget to get out of the way of your own ego sometimes. Even if you have to become a protégé or an understudy — do it. Mike Tyson was on the fast track to an early death on the streets of New York City before meeting famed boxing trainer Cus D'Amato, who saw something in him and changed his life en route to Tyson becoming the heavyweight champion of the boxing world. Arnold Schwarzenegger was a protégé to Joe Weider, the creator of the Mr. Olympia and Ms. Olympia bodybuilding tournaments, among other fitness endeavors.

Every person who has the knowledge you seek can only admire a person who comes to them in sincerity, humility and respect. Be willing and have an open mind to learn from someone who sees the potential to be great in you, even if a part of you has to be harmed in the sense of what you believed in the past was wrong. Make that person your mentor if need be, and make sure their knowledge is relevant to your mission. Remember: no question is foolish. Leverage any beneficial relationship you have to maximize your own success.

When you are acquiring knowledge from whatever source you choose, also consider what's being disseminated. Many nuggets of wisdom born in the past have stood the test of time, while others have been ignored by new generations. Be critical of everything and take nothing at face value. Believe nothing until it's understood by you and clearly proven. Yes, knowledge is power but only when it's useful to you and if you choose to understand based on your experiences. Misinformation can seal your fate before you even truly begin your mission's path. Irrelevant information will get you nowhere and incorrect information breaks down easily, so take and use what you need and toss away the rest. Constantly filter what you read and what you are told to draw useful information, as your time and your mind are precious commodities. Cut out the noise so you can fine tune your mind and your mission. In any case, be careful of the advice you choose to consume.

Sometimes, you don't even need to explicitly seek knowledge from a person related to your mission — just look at how they failed and learn from their mistakes. In essence, you have the experience of yourself and the experience of others. Our own experience is slow, labored, costly and often hard to bear. The experience of others is a ready-made book of directions on knowledge and life, on what to do and what not to do. The observed experience is free of charge. As such, you don't need to suffer their hardships. You can learn from any mistakes they might have made — all you have to do is observe and pay attention.

                                    Becoming Mr. Right

So what to do with all the knowledge, ingrained and/or acquired, that you can use in your mission? Like it was stated in Chapter 2, starting small is the key to success in any endeavor. The reason to start small is to not get ahead of yourself and set yourself up for disappointment. It increases the chances of permanent failure if you feel you are not progressing fast or proficient enough to your liking. It is essential for you, men, to accept and embrace your mission and the long process ahead. Success in anything is not a one-off achievement or born via blind luck — it is a continual and evolving process.

9.
Love The Process

"Do not pray for easy lives. Pray to be stronger men."
— John F. Kennedy

You are bound to face a long, frustrating and difficult journey toward becoming the fulfillment of your mission. But rest assured, the rewards are well worth the struggle. Men, never underestimate the surprising power of frustration, which is a byproduct of passion. This might sound counterintuitive, but frustration will help bring the best out of you, and your definition of success will mean that much more.

To be successful, the first thing to do is fall in love with your work. And just like in the game of love, the trick to staying motivated enough to make it to the top while enjoying every step of the journey in your mission is desire. The more desire you have in your mission, the more determined and focused you will be to get to your finish line and not be permanently defeated by any failure you witness. But how do you maintain your desire throughout the course of your mission?

Start with yourself. The outside world might give you a tough fight, but the greatest enemy a man has is himself. You create your own reality. With that said, most people pack up shop and accept defeat as a form of protection. Those people have no love for themselves or the desire to push through. They choose to sit on the sidelines applauding others for excelling, notably professional athletes, top-selling musicians and award-winning actors, quietly thinking, "That could have been me." What makes the cream rise to the top is embracing the naturally curved road in the process toward a successful mission.

Most people want things in life to go from point A to point B in a straight, short line full of shortcuts and lucky breaks. There are no GPS or smartphone navigation apps on the road of your mission. The only thing you know most days is the destination you are going toward. Pit stops and breakdowns could be common occurrences on your road, but having the passion to not retreat and revisit the place you are attempting to leave behind forever should be the fuel you need to keep pressing forward.

The worst mistake you can make is to think you can't make mistakes. If you make a mistake, don't have the whip ready to commit proverbial self-flagellation. Every time you unnecessarily criticize or say something harsh to yourself, it depletes you of your energy and drive, leading to depression and doubt.

Allow yourself to be imperfect and learn to be gentle with yourself when you make a mistake so you don't become your own worst enemy. Don't be ready to throw away the proverbial book over one mistake, just turn the page to a new chapter in your journey. The biggest mistake you can believe is not believing you can make any. It's OK to make mistakes; they are only fatal if you let them become fatal. You'll never stop making mistakes. What's important is to try and learn from those, so you don't keep repeating them.

Desire is an expensive commodity; it can't be forced, bought, or negotiated. If you have desire in anything in life, you will not make excuses or stories about why you can't do certain things or go certain places. Desire helps you stem the tides of disappointment and false starts. Desire is channeling your energies to find ways to make things happen in your mission, instead of trying to catch butterflies with a tennis racket.

Having the desire to find a mission and continue on is a matter of having the right attitude. Attitude can matter more than ability or even will. You will go nowhere without the proper attitude.

Mind you, attitude is not a fleeting emotion. Your emotions are not you, and your emotions only define you if you let them. Accept emotions for what they are — a part of your life — and then continue to press forward in your mission. Let your attitude dictate your emotions, not the other way around. Attitude is a state of mind and a continual process of being.

No matter what mission you choose to pursue, there are risks special to it. There's always the chance to succeed and to fail. No matter what side of the coin falls, a key is to have motivation based on the concept of "always process." That doesn't mean to look forward in place of appreciating today, but the "always process" means that no matter if you fail or succeed in your endeavors, you have the attitude of consistently not resting on your victories or defeats and always moving forward. You're always trying to improve in some arena. You're always trying to compete for what you want. You're always trying to stay ahead of the curve and the competition. You're always aware of people trying to kick your butt and set you back. And you're always trying to kick your own butt into gear before someone else does. It's no different from trying to retain or repeat as champion in a sport.

Another aspect to fortifying desire is realizing that you are finite. Sorry to sound dour, but one day you will die, like we all

                                          Becoming Mr. Right

will. The goal in life is to create something that will physically outlive you — whether it's having a family and children, creating the next great invention, a book that will be read long after you've passed, forging public policy that will help others for years, spreading ideas and concepts that will stand the test of time, etc. The most important thing a man needs to realize is that your time is valuable to others, and to yourself. Internalize this, men: Time is a man's most valuable resource. Use your desire to be self-aware and spend it wisely. For every second, minute and hour you're investing in your mission, be sure you're getting a return — that could be in the people you meet, the skills you acquire, the connections you make, the work you create or anything that is of value to you. You can always make more money or opportunities, but you can never make more time.

Also, don't expect to change overnight. Overnight success is a dangerous myth. You didn't get in the predicament you want to change overnight, so don't expect change to happen at the same rate. If you feel like you're trying too hard, then you're trying too hard — it's that simple, yet so hard to grasp fully when you are in the slog of change, sort to speak. The race to fulfillment is not a sprint against an Olympic gold medalist runner.

Struggling is part of your mission and it makes victory a whole lot sweeter. Sometimes, you have to love the process more than you love the result. The result is sometimes unclear but the process is in your face every single day. If you can't love what you do day to day, you just won't reach your destination.

10.
Embrace
The Struggle

"Strength does not come from winning. Your struggles develop your strengths. When you go through hardships and decide not to surrender, that is strength."
— Arnold Schwarzenegger

So you have a mission in mind and are taking the steps necessary to make in fulfilling. Hopefully, you'll not struggle and falter badly — but that happens to the best of us, as long as you don't take any losses to heart and become bitter, jaded and disillusioned. Defeat is not final unless you give up without giving it your all.

The struggle in anything you do in your life will fortify your resolve to accomplish your mission. You will fail along the way, trust me. Failure is OK and is part of the process, as long as you let any failures become temporary, not permanent. Most of the time, you'll learn more by losing than you do by winning.

Failure is a cornerstone on the road to success; for every

failure, you become more experienced. If you learn from these failures, you will never be a failure. Never forget the lessons that failures can teach you. This is all a part of the process of your mission. This might sound counterintuitive, but to succeed you need those failures to learn from. After failing, you gain a certain hindsight that gives you clarity about your actions and what can do differently the next time.

You might be fearless — but that could set you up for failure. Any endeavor no matter the size will make you question yourself — it's only a natural reaction. Sometimes being fearless can amount to hubris, telling yourself that nothing can stop you. That might me true, but your fears can be used to your benefit. Know what your fears are and you can work through them one by one.

Fight the fear and don't let it paralyze you or make you second guess yourself; it's probably not even a reality. Channel your fear and let it work for you, not against you. You should not be ruled by false evidence appearing real. Negative emotions are a necessary part of life. As such, they should be managed and learned from, not avoided. Having doubts is not necessarily a bad thing, mind you — those feelings can help pave the path you're on by giving you pause to see if you are on the right track.

Recognize that you might have the same fears surface over and over again. As such, you can develop techniques to deal with them, like exercise to expend nervous energy or to write them down to let them escape from your mind. As I said in chapter, two, you can be your own worst enemy most days. Be gracious with yourself and know you are going to fail.

With all those previous words being said about emotions, it could be easy to stay trapped in your head and become anxious or unsure. Taking action trumps thinking about taking action. It should behoove you to get out of your own head sometimes and just feel things out. Men are analytical by nature and we like to go over a lot of processes, hypotheses and possibilities. None of those potential mental hurdles can be overcome unless you take positive action. Positive action is greater than positive thinking. Positive action is the building block to success. It can build for you a curve of momentum, clearer focus on the process of your mission, and can lend you to find ways to get excited and motivated each day. Action isn't an option, men — it's a requirement.

Embracing the struggle is appreciating all of the ups and downs in the process. Every up and every down is a learning experience. Use your ups to recognize what you're doing right and aim to keep the momentum going; use your downs to learn what went wrong and how you can correct your steps. Embrace the struggle that your mission might give you. Think of struggle as a barrier that will keep others from achieving the mastery you will achieve if you just keep at it. Mastery of anything brings true enjoyment, and mastery can only be enjoyed by fighting through the plateaus that are sure to formulate.

Also realize that trying and failing a mission will often give you a great moment of clarity about yourself. Every moment of being uncomfortable is brining you closer to being great in your mission. Even in failure, men, you'll notice you have certain aptitudes that might not help with your chosen mission, but might be better suited for another mission you choose to pursue.

The struggle and the suffering is an indicator of growth if you choose to accept it as such. The win-at-all-costs mindset of your mission can make any breakdowns you might undertake as your breakthrough.

Here's a scenario for you to ponder: A baby begins teething and is in discomfort as his first teeth begin protruding from his gums. There is certain and obvious pain, through buckets of drool or buckets of tears. But when the first tooth makes its appearance, the baby is used to the pain and gains a sort of comfort and acclimation in waiting for the next tooth to debut.

As people, we like things the easy way where the possibility of pain and discomfort is next to nothing. That's a mistake. Pain and discomfort is where growth and progress occur. You can't have one without the other. Every aspect of growth brings about a little death of the old you. You have to die sometimes before you can live.

Growth and progress in your mission and in life in general happens over time; it should never come easy. If it does, it might give you a false sense of accomplishment. Rome wasn't built in a day, and neither are you and what you are working to become. Welcome the roadblocks and speed bumps you are sure to encounter, as they give you a chance to re-evaluate how things are going and if things need a slight tweak or a general overhaul. Use every life experience, regardless of the pleasure or drudgery, to prepare you for where you are right now and what is to come in the future.

Whether you are far along or in the beginning stages of your mission, expanding your circle of authenticity can be a beneficial way to stay consistent and become an example for others to see, and hopefully emulate.

11.
Expanding Your Inner Circle

*"Life isn't about finding yourself.
Life is about creating yourself."*
— G.B. Shaw

The path in your mission starts out as a solitary affair, but can be made or broken by the relationships you foster. Surrounding yourself with those who bring out the best in you, not the stress in you, can take you over the top in your life. It's necessary that you get the naysayers and losers out of your life if you want to live your mission. It's is also necessary to aid the people who support you and your mission in your life — as long as it comes from a place of authenticity.

No man is an island, and you can't win most of the games in life by yourself. Michael Jordan was an up-and-coming force for the Chicago Bulls, but he needed Scottie Pippen and head coach Phil Jackson to help cement his individual legacy and win six NBA championships in eight seasons.

The people you meet influence what you learn, what you believe and what you can become. Every person you meet has something to teach you. As you progress in life, your inner circle gets expanded. By paying attention to your relationships and the types of people you let in your inner circle, you can upgrade or downgrade any progress. In many cases, your performance in certain areas of your life as well can be affected. Improving existing relationships, adding new relationships or eliminating unproductive or unhealthy relationships can have a dramatic impact on your mission and your life. A key aspect to personal success is building the right team around you.

In Chapter 7, I discussed belief, primarily in you. It's fine to go it alone, but along your journey, you might need a helping hand or someone you can safely and without judgment confide in about the ups and downs of life. A man can be made or broken by the people closest to him. Your relationships should be making you a better person. Wisely expand you inner circle for these three reasons:

● **For feedback.** Trust and ask for advice from people with a proven, successful track record in their espoused discipline. You need people who will be honest and supportive of you. Surround yourself with people you trust who will champion you to be who you are aiming to be. The people you associate with can reflect back on you to gauge how you are doing so you can improve yourself and stay on course. The people in our lives can also challenge us to continue, to keep moving forward and to correct us if we are getting off track. Your inner circle should have the purpose of giving honest and respectful feedback to help you progress and grow. Use the opinions of your peers and those close to you for feedback if they align with your mission. In the end, the only opinion of yourself that should matter to you is your own.

• **For companionship.** To help better yourself, you need to have better people around you — whether they are family, friends or other associates. Align yourself with those who are just as passionate if not more passionate than you. People in your inner circle should support, inspire, uplift and challenge you for the better. Cherish those who benefit you in any way. For people who belittle, downplay, hurt or bring you down in any way, excise them like a cancer. It's OK to give them a second chance if you choose, but free passes are not allowed. Like author and motivational speaker Tony Gaskins Jr. says, "You are the CEO of your life, and all the hiring and firing decisions with people who help or hinder you are yours to make." Avoid sad, angry, unhappy, bitter and unsuccessful people. If their lives are not in order, what could you possibly learn from them besides how not to live?

• **For control.** Another key to your circle is having complete control over how big or small it can be and how close certain people can be to your center, as some relationships can be closer than others. Your inner circle should be handled and maintained with great care and vigilance. The relationships in your inner circle are relationships of your choosing, and must be chosen carefully. The key is to live in your own reality and have the skill and ability to let people come and go based on your rules, not theirs.

One simple exercise you can do is to go back to your days in elementary or primary school art class. Draw a circle with your name in the center of it. From there, put the names of people you hold dear outside of it. Draw circles around their names and draw a line from each respective name to the center circle. This is a crude but effective manifestation of your universe. You can add people when you feel the connections are strong and you erase people at your behest when you feel they are subtracting from you.

The benefits for expanding or contracting your circle as needed are tremendous. If you choose to take control of the relationships you form and foster, and you will have taken a step in charge of your life. When you seek people, don't ask for a handout — ask to gain some wisdom and insight from people you want to have in your life.

Crafting your inner circle takes throwing away old ways of seeking people to add, but using your value to redefine the people you surround yourself with. In your mission's journey, you are seeking to transform yourself in all matters. For better or for worse, you are setting standards for yourself that branch out to all aspects of your life. In the manner of self-improvement, you need to raise your standards involving everyone in your life.

12.
New Life, New Standards

"If you don't set a baseline standard for what you'll accept in life, you'll find it's easy to slip into behaviors and attitudes or a quality of life that's far below what you deserve."
— Tony Robbins

By now, your old life and what was in it is a distant memory. The new life you are creating must have new standards for success. Actively setting new standards is about respecting yourself and respecting what you want in your life. Having standards help sets you apart from the herd. When you do not have any set standards or if your standards are not good enough in relation to your current life, then you will not fully attain your chosen mission and the goals in your life. Standards are the measurements that will help you assess the sum of your life and its meaning.

The mission you choose and the results you attain should bleed over into all aspects of your life — and that's because of

the new standards you set for yourself. Having new standards
for yourself will force growth and increase your potential for
success. When you expect more from yourself, you get more for
yourself — emotionally, financially, physically, mentally and
spiritually. If you are not willing to improve these very basic and
straightforward aspects of your life and accept nothing but the
best for yourself, you then have no business complaining about
the results. There is no reason to settle for anything inadequate
in your life through having little or no standards.

The standards in your life should rotate around your physical
and mental health, relationships (family, friends, co-workers),
routines, habits, activities, etc. Think of it in this manner: I like
to have a clean house, where I know where everything is at all
times. Call me a neat freak, but I like things to have a place.
I can't stand messy homes, as in my opinion it is an outward
display of internal conditions. Residents of messy homes might
make excuses for why they can't clean up, but if they set a new
standard of cleanliness, then the mess can be transformed into a
miracle.

Having new standards means pushing yourself for more —
to achieve more, to ask for more, to claim what you believe is
yours. Holding yourself to new high standards is important and
integral for you. Also, this also translates to the standards you
set for others in your life.

Yes, setting new standards for others in your life seems counterintuitive at first glance, as you can't control what other people
do in your presence. What I mean by holding others to standards
is not related to expectations, but what you deem as acceptable to your worldview. If you choose to hold yourself to high
standards, then that results in you holding others accountable to
high standards as well. As soon as you settle for second or third
best in anything and anyone, that is what you will receive. Your

self-respect and reputation are on the line if you accept less than the best for yourself.

In setting new standards for yourself and for others, you are making yourself into a magnet. That personal magnet will attract into your life the people, relationships, jobs, money and opportunities that will be in alignment with the standards you set and keep for yourself.

Just like having standards that are low is detrimental, standards that are too high are a cause for concern as well. Setting unrealistic standards in both extremes can do more harm than good, unnecessarily setting you up for failure with yourself and others.

For better or worse, men are defined by the standards they set for themselves and for others. Having a newly constructed power of high standards inside you is for your benefit, but can also be used to improve the lives of others. People give to others for various reasons — out of joyous service, nagging guilt, social or religious obligations or pitiful supplication. The choice to give and be an example to others should be a choice born of strength, not of weakness.

13.
A New Way To Give

"We need to learn to love ourselves first, in all our glory and our imperfections. If we cannot love ourselves, we cannot fully open to our ability to love others or our potential to create. Evolution and all hopes for a better world rest in the fearlessness and open-hearted vision of people who embrace life."
— John Lennon

Men who have found their mission in life and are actively working toward that are attractive to people. Like it or not, your internal workings are being broadcast to the world the second you leave your home. The best way to give, the only way to give as a matter of fact, is through being authentic and genuine. Simply conveying your 100 percent real, genuine, authentic, and vulnerable self when you are with others shows massive charisma, confidence, competence and self-assurance — which are all expressed through action.

There is a term I'd like to introduce you to — it's called

"abundance mentality." What is abundance mentality? Introduced in Stephen R. Covey's best-selling book "The Seven Habits of Highly Effective People," abundance mentality is a concept in which a person believes there are enough physical and mental resources and successes to share with others. Also, this mentality means the ambitions one exhibits helps fuel the fire of the self. This also means that if you experience failure in your life, you will have the confidence to assuredly find success in courtship, business, your personal life, etc.

As a man, having an abundance mentality is an important truth during one's self development, as opposed to having a "scarcity mentality," where you have a mindset that there are a limited and finite amount of resources and successes you can obtain and share with others. Men with a scarcity mentality, like I was at one time, are afraid of loss, shame and embarrassment. As such, he'll tread carefully and not push the issue in his dealings. His vision narrows to the point he doesn't see opportunity, mostly because he's focusing his energies on staying on guard to not fall. Both the abundance and scarcity mentalities are a state of mind that is formed through your experiences, both the good and the bad.

To be of value to others, you must give something of value. Makes sense, right? At a certain point, you should formulate a new way to give back, based on the knowledge, experiences and values you have acquired in the course of your mission. As a result, you could become a vital source of value and enrichment to others you deem worthy of your energies. In doing so, you can create relationships and benefit the lives of others on your terms.

In some cases, people might come to you for advice or a helping hand. Don't recoil at this possibility — embrace it. Cowardice is a decision, and so is service. Serve your purpose and not your fears. Most people who ask others for help have a need to gain courage in their convictions. The gift of courage through your words and actions is a great gift to give to others, so give it out on your terms. If you choose to speak on something, speak with passion and conviction. Even if you are wrong through their skewed perspective, people are sure to gain respect for you for standing up and having conviction for something.

Men on a mission are men of high value — and many people know that. High-value men know things that others want and need to know. There are many ways to offer your value to worthy people and causes. And the more you help others, the more you are going to help yourself. Be warned, however — don't let people latch themselves to you like a leech, even if you're not at the high value you are working toward. Here are some ways to give of yourself to others you classify as worthy of your value:

• **Give your time.** As stated in Chapter 9, the most important resource a man has is not his body or his paycheck, but his time. Men might be an expendable cog in society's machine, but you have the choice of where and with whom to spend your time. That is a choice that should not be taken lightly, but with much deliberation and thought as possible. You can recover lost money or items, but never your time. Spending time with people who care for you and who you care for, or volunteering at an event, house of worship, or club can enhance the lives of others, bringing them and yourself value.

• **Give your resources.** In giving your resources, I mean of the things that are visible, like money, clothes, physical skills, food, hobbies, etc., and things that cannot be seen, like knowledge, social status, etc. No matter what resources are at your disposal, they can be used to help others. If there is something you are well-versed in or an expert on, trying to find someone less knowledgable to share it with can help you pay forward the knowledge you were given by others in your mission. Making an impact on someone's life, whether family, friend or stranger, is a highly valued and sought-after aspect of masculinity. To do so enriches our lives as well and can entrench a man further in his mission. Everyone benefits from giving and being the recipient of gifts by authentic people.

• **Give your spirit.** Like I said earlier, time is a man's most precious resource. Coinciding with that is your energy and drive. Some men are extroverts and love being around people. Giving of their spirit is natural and easy to them, as they seem to have their batteries recharged in an instant. Other men, like me, are introverts that are selective in whom they give themselves to, as their batteries need a little longer to get back to full capacity. In both cases, the energy we choose to give out is reciprocated by those with whom we associate. You can't help but feel good when you receive a friendly wave hello, a smile, a hug, a kiss or any other physical sign of appreciation or affection when you give. I'm a physically affectionate person, so I love hugs — that is a sign I'm being appreciated and loved. Ladies, that's my love language, by the way. It sounds cliché, but when you give, you're more likely to get back. And when we give to others, it connects you to each other so that when they feel closer to you, you also feel closer to them.

• **Give your gratitude.** As much as you might not like to admit it, you get helped along the way to meeting your mission. Having a feeling of gratitude is is good to have in ourselves and is an energy that can be easily transferred to others. Being grateful forces you to slow down and take in what you have earned through your actions or have been gifted by others. The more you are grateful, the more you discover what you have to be grateful for. Gratitude trains your mind to focus on the things and people that matter to you in life. Gratitude helps you recognize other people's favors to you.

                                   Becoming Mr. Right

Do your part to sincerely thank those who have done well by you not only through your words, but more importantly through your actions. And as corny as it sounds, the more you give the more you get. By having a spirit of gratitude, you are more apt to support others with their problems or assist them in a time of need. People like being appreciated for who they are and what they do — especially if it's been of benefit to you. It costs you little to show gratitude, and it's a selfless way to make someone else happy. And making someone else happy will bring benefit to you. Never underestimate the power you give to someone by believing in them, assisting them and inspiring them.

With all the aforementioned ways to give, you must have something to give in order to give it away. That seems simplistic but it's true, at least in my experiences. The energy to give must first originate in yourself, and pursuing your mission is the best way to cultivate your energies. In this world, there is no shortage of ways and avenues to give of your time, services and energy to causes or people you deem worthy of yourself. You will be of greatest service to the world if you spend time doing things you enjoy, that you are good at, and that you are happiest doing.

Building yourself in the image of your mission and passions, giving yourself to those whom you see fit, and leaving a legacy in your wake are badges of what it should mean to be a man. Despite the definition of masculinity being changed with each generation, some old truths still transcend time and scrutiny.

No matter the path you take, just know that the ride will be long, full of multiple lanes, bumps, roadblocks and speed traps along the way. In the same vein, you will be in full control of how you drive, determining your ultimate destination and the length of your journey.

14.
The Journey Never Ends

"There are hundreds of paths up the mountain, all leading to the same place, so it doesn't matter which path you take. The only person wasting time is the one who runs around the mountain, telling everyone that his or her path is wrong."
— Hindu proverb

The journey your mission will take you on will be the best ride of your life, like the biggest, longest roller coaster you ever rode. Your mission is essentially a journey of self-discovery, about finding out more about yourself, trying out many different things and finally focusing on the actions and people that give you life. There's always more for you to discover. Over time, your interests might shift and what used to be your mission no longer is. That's OK; it's a part of being human.

In the end, it always comes down to doing what you love and

creating a life that feels good to you on the inside, not one that just looks good on the outside. When you feel a deep sense of satisfaction about what you're doing with your life, you have found your mission. You will be a beacon of light and positivity to others, like the brightest star in the dark midnight sky.

It's never too late to change your life for the better — no matter your age, race, sexual orientation, economic status, family situation, geography, etc. I used to let my past define my future — no more to that backward way of thinking. The worst part of backward thinking is using the past as a self-imposed weight on your shoulders. I foolishly let my past define my future. When I realized that I had control of my life — not my past or my circumstances — a great power came over me, like I was alive for the first time, not just existing and taking up space and oxygen.

The same goes with you, men; your past isn't your future and you can change the narrative in your story anytime you want. Yes, the past happened; you can't control that. But your past isn't your destiny. It's all about how you frame your mind, which will carry downward through the rest of your body and into your spirit. You can choose to play the victim or the victor over your circumstances. You can control yourself now and in the future. Men, ask yourself this: Are you doing what you need to do today to get you closer to where you want to be tomorrow?

The only guarantee is life is that it will end. Life also gives us no guarantee of continuous comfort or peace. What life guarantees us are uncertainties, insecurities and disorder. On the inverse of these negatives are the positive construction of inner-strength, the discovery of your character and multiple opportunities for personal growth. Those aforementioned opportunities can only be revealed to men who are ready, observant and faithful to his mission. In the end, to take responsibility for both their current circumstances and also for the direction they wish to traverse is a hallmark of a man.

You, men, have the power to build, reinvent or repair yourself today. The time and the place you are reading this is just a temporary moment in your life that can be emboldened with the right mindset, steadfast work ethic and well-placed hope for the future. There is a way to take hold of your life, whether for the first time or for another trip down the road of self-improvement and actualization.

Being a male is a matter of birth, but being a man is a matter of choice. Men are builders, protectors, providers, fighters and conquerors. The only limits you have on yourself are the ones you mentally and spiritually put there. The time to become the man you want to be is right now!

A poem from English playwright John Fletcher, "The Honest Man's Fortune," is a fitting element to help conclude this book. A man has the awesome power, responsibility and duty to craft his life and the destiny of himself and those he chooses to bring into it:

> "Man is his own star; and the soul that can
> Render an honest and a perfect man,
> Commands all light, all influence, all fate;
> Nothing to him falls early or too late.
> Our acts our angels are, or good or ill,
> Our fatal shadows that walk by us still."

Men — it's time to build the best version of yourself for yourself. Don't wait until an arbitrary date, event, or the start of a new calendar year — begin the process now. All of your dreams can come true, but only if you have the courage, confidence and competency to pursue them — all you have to do is believe in it and in yourself. I certainly am with my dreams.

It's a long, hard road to your destiny and every step could get progressively heavier, but it will be worth it when fulfillment and your definition of success has been achieved. You should not want it any other way. Let these words from my continuing journey spark real internal change in your lives, men.

Throughout this book, I hope you've learned that you have complete and total control over yourself; all the good and all the bad. This book will be worthless to if you don't at least try to put many of its contents in action in the real world. Taking action is better than thinking about taking action and all the machinations therein.

Radio personality Tom Leykis is credited as saying, "There's some benefit to being happy in your life. Of looking around and saying, 'This is mine.' " Find what you love to do and brings you happiness and fulfillment, then own it and be the absolute best you can be at it — whether it's being the best writer, best musician, best businessman, best athlete, best lover, best father, best husband, best public servant, best soldier, best doctor, best whatever. Along the way, don't forget to reflect on the journey you have chosen to undertake and the positive people who are witnessing your life.

Everything in life after you are born is made from the choices you make. Every choice you make is first born in your mind, and as you think you shall become. Do you choose to be a victim of your circumstances or do you choose to build the life you want? Do not let your future be limited by your past experiences. Never underestimate the power you give yourself by believing in you. Make the conscious choice to build and to always strive forward in progress.

The world is waiting on you.

About the Author

Eric S. Gillard and his love of reading and the written word go back to his days as a child, using them as an escape and refuge. He parlayed that love into a Bachelor's degree in English from Christopher Newport University in Newport News, Va.

After graduating in 2005, he turned his internship with the Daily Press, his hometown newspaper, into a job as a copy editor and page designer.

He transferred to reporting and won a first-place award for best story/picture combination from the Virginia Press Association in 2009 for a five-part series on the homeless on the Virginia Peninsula, besting bigger papers like the Washington Post, Virginian-Pilot and Richmond Times-Dispatch.

He has three nieces and a nephew whom he considers his children until he gets some of his own with the right girl.

When he's not working or spending family time, he can be found running, at the beach, or enjoying a fancy cheeseburger with a cider.

www.ingramcontent.com/pod-product-compliance
Lightning Source LLC
Chambersburg PA
CBHW071503030726
47593CB00003B/1131